The Friendship Book

by Dr. Katie O'Connell, Ph.D., and Lynn Huggins-Cooper

ARCTURUS

ARCTURUS

This edition published in 2021 by Arcturus Publishing Limited
26/27 Bickels Yard, 151–153 Bermondsey Street,
London SE1 3HA

Copyright © Arcturus Holdings Limited

Authors: Dr. Katie O'Connell, Ph.D., and Lynn Huggins-Cooper
Illustrator: Stef Murphy
Editor: Violet Peto
Designer: Stefan Holliland
Managing Editor: Joe Harris

ISBN: 978-1-3988-1443-1
CH008352NT
Supplier 29, Date 0821, Print run 10789

Printed in China

Contents

Finding Friendship 4

Helping Hands 6

Well, Hello There! 8

Survey the Scene 10

Find Your Tribe............................... 12

Feeling Left Out............................... 14

Lights, Camera, Action! 16

Mapping Friendship 18

Friendship Soup............................... 20

Friends Come in All Shapes and Sizes 22

Comfortable Conversations 24

All Ears... 26

Pay Attention! 28

Bodies Talk! 30

Joining In.. 32

Conversations Count........................ 34

Great Groups 36

One to One 38

Just Joking!..................................... 40

Asking Questions 42

Great Games 44

Find the Clues 46

Interesting Invitations 48

What If?.. 50

Helping Friendships Grow 52

Sharing Is Caring............................. 54

Show Sympathy............................... 56

Actions and Reactions 58

What Would You Do? 60

Why Did They Do That?................... 62

Oops! Sorry 64

Keeping Calm 66

Solving Problems Together 68

Friendship Library........................... 70

Playing by the Rules........................ 72

Develop Your Kindness Muscles 74

Caring Compliments........................ 76

Have Empathy 78

When Friendships Fade 80

Friendship Checklist 82

Friendship High Five 84

For Parents

   Why does my child find it hard

   to make friends?............................ 86

   How you can help........................... 88

Glossary 94

Further Reading 95

Index.. 96

Finding Friendship

Friendship is a wonderful thing—friends can brighten our days, and fill our lives with love and laughter. Sometimes, it can be hard to make friends when you aren't sure how to make the first move. This book can help you to work through any worries you have about making friends. The activities will give you practical ideas about how and where to find the right friends for you, as well as how to be a good friend to others.

Make yourself comfortable in a snug, calm place and take a look through this book. There are ideas to read and activities to do, so you might like to make sure you have your crayons with you. You can do the activities once, twice, or many times. It's up to you! You can do them in any order, so look for things that interest you or activities that feel like they would help you right now, whatever is worrying you about friendship.

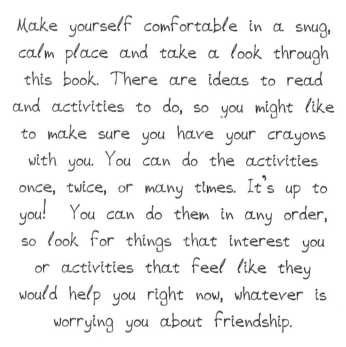

Who can help you?

If you feel lonely, or anxious about making friends, remember that you do not have to cope alone. Learning to make friends and manage friendships is a part of growing up. You may be able to talk to your parents, guardians, grandparents, teachers, or even older brothers or sisters. Talking about your worries and hearing about how other people make and keep friends will help you to understand what to do. If you are feeling anxious, find a person you trust and let them know.

Helping Hands

Finding really kind people who like to help others is a good
way to make friends.

In a group, look for "helpers." In the playground, they may be helping
people on play equipment. In class, they might help others to do their
work or find what they need. These kind people are often really
friendly, and making friends with them will help you to get to know
the rest of the group.

When someone helps someone else to join in, it's like giving them a gift. Each time you notice someone helping, write what they did on one of these gift tags. This will help you to recognize helpers—and learn how to be one! Helpful people make friends because they are kind.

How it helps

Finding a helper will ease your entry into a group. Helpers are usually good at reading people and confident in tricky situations. By watching them, you can learn how to act and what to say. Can you think of a good friendship role model?

Well, Hello There!

Do you know how to say hello to new people? Recognizing kind greetings and looking friendly yourself will help you to make friends more easily.

Knowing how to say hello to people you don't know can be hard if you are feeling shy! Watch how friends say hello to each other each day.

Do they smile and look into each other's eyes?

Do they use their friends' names when they say hi to them?

Nice to meet you.

My name is …

I'm new here.

Hi there!

Hello.

Now try out ways to say hello. Imagine you are meeting a person for the first time. Try the different greetings in these speech bubbles. Which "hello" feels most comfortable?

If you remember to smile, it will give people the signal that you want to be friends. It can be hard to smile when you are feeling nervous, so try and think of things that make you happy. It might be your pet or a game you like to play. Thinking happy thoughts will help your face to look warm and friendly when meeting new people.

How it helps

A friendly greeting and a warm smile are clues that someone is kind and wants to be friends. Watch for these clues in other people—and remember that people are looking for your clues, too. Be sure to smile and say hello, so that people know you are a nice, friendly person.

Survey the Scene

Look for friendship in lots of places, and you will soon build a collection of friendly faces.

You can find friends in all kinds of places—not just at school. Think about all the places you can meet people—sports clubs, hobby groups, playing near your home, or at the park. What other places can you think of?

Draw pictures of two different places you might find friends on these friendship binoculars.

Joining clubs that interest you means that you will meet people who share that interest. It might be a quiet, gentle club like an art club, or it could be a lively, active sports club. No matter what club you join, there will be people there you can talk to because you are interested in the same things. That makes it easier to start a conversation because you can talk about the things you are doing.

How it helps

Sometimes it is easier to talk to people when you have a reason to talk—like asking how to do something or showing someone how to use equipment. Clubs can help you find friends in safe spaces where you share interests.

Find Your Tribe!

Finding friends is easiest when you have lots of things in common—but having differences is great, too!

When you are looking for friends, it is important to find people who accept you for the person you are. There's no point in trying to force yourself into a group that isn't a good fit for you. Instead, look for people who are like you in some way. If you find the things you have in common, you have something to share.

Circle all the things that these children have in common. Do you think they would be good friends for one another?

Name: Freya Qualities	Name: Daleep Qualities	Name: Aleena Qualities
Kind	Kind	Kind
Does not like sports	Loves tennis	Likes sport
Imaginative	Imaginative	Imaginative
Likes cooking	Loves dogs	Loves animals
Loves cats	Loves computer games	Likes computer games
Loves arts and crafts	Good at writing stories	Likes arts and crafts

Now make your own list using people you know. Try and figure out who has things in common that might make them friends.

Having things in common with others forms the foundation of friendships, but friends can still have lots of differences. In fact, difference is one of the things that makes people interesting. We all need others to have fun with—but we can have different personalities, backgrounds, and hobbies, and still be great friends.

How it helps

Thinking about the things people have in common helps us to see that it doesn't matter if we look different when it comes to being friends.

Feeling Left Out

Feeling like everyone is part of a friendship group apart from you can be difficult, so here are some ways to join in.

It's hard not to feel left out when everyone else seems to be having fun playing a game. But what do you do if you don't know everyone? How can you become part of the group? First of all, watch the game they are playing and see what's happening. If there are natural breaks in the game, that might be a good time to join in. Talk to a friendly looking person, and ask if you can play, too. But don't be too sad if they say no. If you practice what to say if the answer is no, you'll feel more confident.

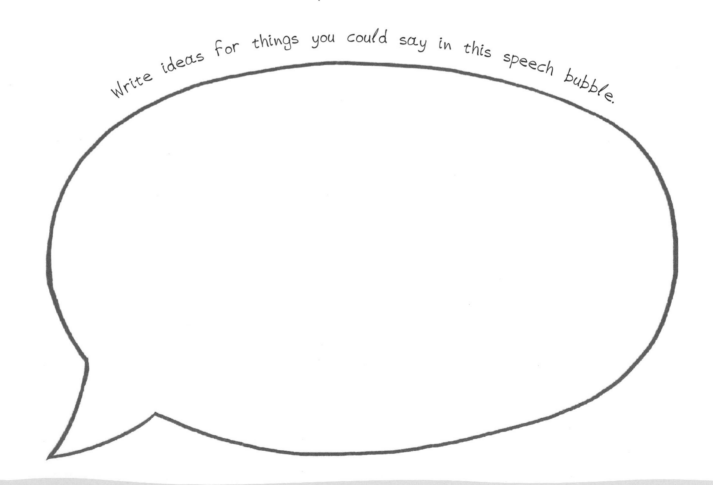

Write ideas for things you could say in this speech bubble.

If you are not allowed to join in right away, that doesn't mean the group want to leave you out. It could be that the game is in full flow, and you joining at that moment would stop the action as you caught up with what was going on. Instead, maybe ask "Can I play in the next game?" to give people the chance to finish what they are doing, but still include you. Keep watching the action, and you will have a better idea of how to play when you do get to join in.

How it helps

It helps to prepare yourself for "no" answers sometimes. If you are ready for it, you will feel less disappointed and more able to cope without getting upset or cross.

Lights, Camera: Action!

Understanding how games work can make you feel braver.

Watching the action before you join in with a game can make you feel more confident because you know what to do. If you are worried about joining in, take time to watch for a while. Imagine you are making a movie in your head. Which "character" in the film would you like to play with most? Taking this time before you join in can help you to feel safe and calm.

Think about a game you would like to play. Imagine what it would be like to play the game with other people. How would the action play out? Draw some ideas in the film reel.

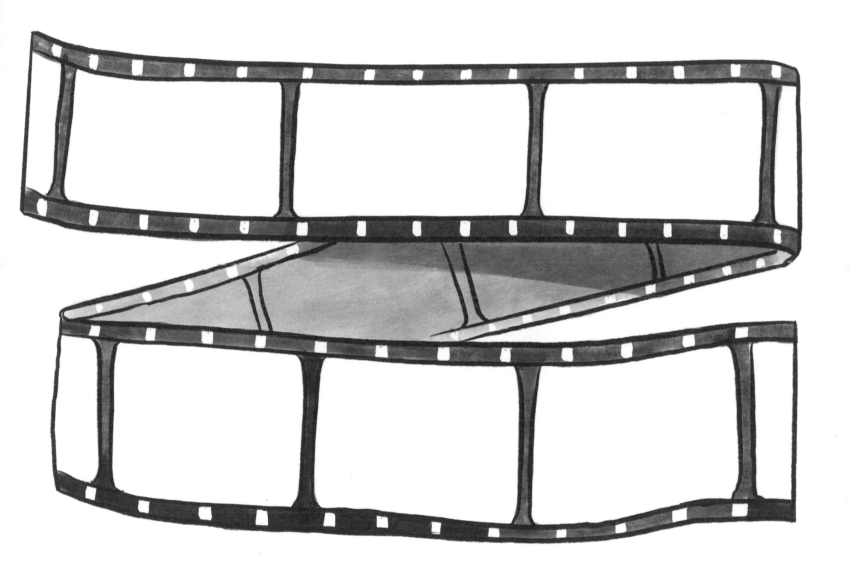

How it helps

It is normal to feel shy in new places and with new people. Learning to relax and watch a situation can make you feel less anxious. Thinking about ways to join in and imagining ways to play will help you to feel more confident.

Mapping Friendship

How do friendships develop? It helps you to make friends if you go in the right direction!

If you think about the journey of friendship, it might help you to understand how friendships work. There isn't just one way for a friendship to develop, but having a map of things to look for can help you recognize friendship as it grows.

The journey of a friendship

Meet at the playground

Smile

Talking

Play together

Share a snack

Agree to meet again

How it helps

Imagining how a friendship might develop step by step can help you to relax and make friends. Planning things out in your head makes it less scary. In real life, things might happen a little differently, but that's part of the fun of friendship—they are all different.

Imagine your own new friendship journey. Draw your ideas on this map along the pathway. Seeing a picture of a friendship journey in your head can help make it feel like something that can happen in real life.

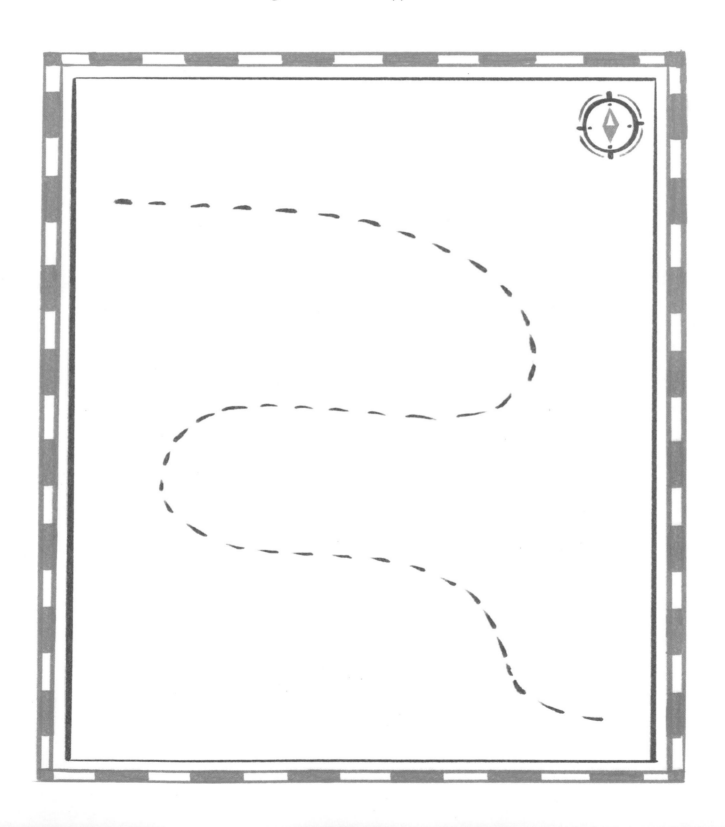

Friendship Soup

The tastiest soup has lots of different ingredients. Friendship is like that, too!

Look at this bowl of soup. The ingredients are all part of friendship. Circle the ingredients that are most important to you in a friend.

If you were writing a recipe for the best friendship you can think of, what qualities would you include? Think about things you like about your friends and include them.

Friendship Recipe

Write your recipe on this page, using lots of ingredients!

How it helps

Thinking about what makes a good friend will help you to be a good friend yourself. We need to be a good friend to others as much as we need good friends ourselves. Friends help support each other when things are tough and make the world a safer, happier place.

Friends Come in All Shapes and Sizes

You don't need to have just one group of friends—you can have different friends for different parts of your life.

You can make friends for different reasons. For example, you could have one friend you do a particular activity with, like tennis. You might not see them much apart from that—and if that suits both of you, it's fine. Maybe you have another friend that is really good at making you laugh and is always fun. That's fine, too.

Friends can be like a beautiful bunch of different types of flowers. One friend does not have to do *all* the jobs a friend can do—in fact, that sounds like too much hard work for one person! Instead, *all* our friends can offer us different things.

Imagine this bunch of flowers was a group of friends. All together, they make a beautiful display. Now, make the flowers as bright as you can with your pencils.

How it helps

Knowing that we can have different friends for different reasons helps us to understand that one friend does not have to do everything. Asking one person to be wonderful at everything creates too much pressure and can make friendships collapse.

Comfortable Conversations

Talking to new people can make you feel nervous or uncomfortable—but there are ways to make it better.

If you are feeling awkward, there's just a chance that the new people you are meeting feel that way, too. Try to imagine how they are feeling. Are they nervous or anxious? Thinking about the way other people are feeling can help you feel calm. You become the "helper" as you try to make them feel more relaxed, and that can make you feel braver.

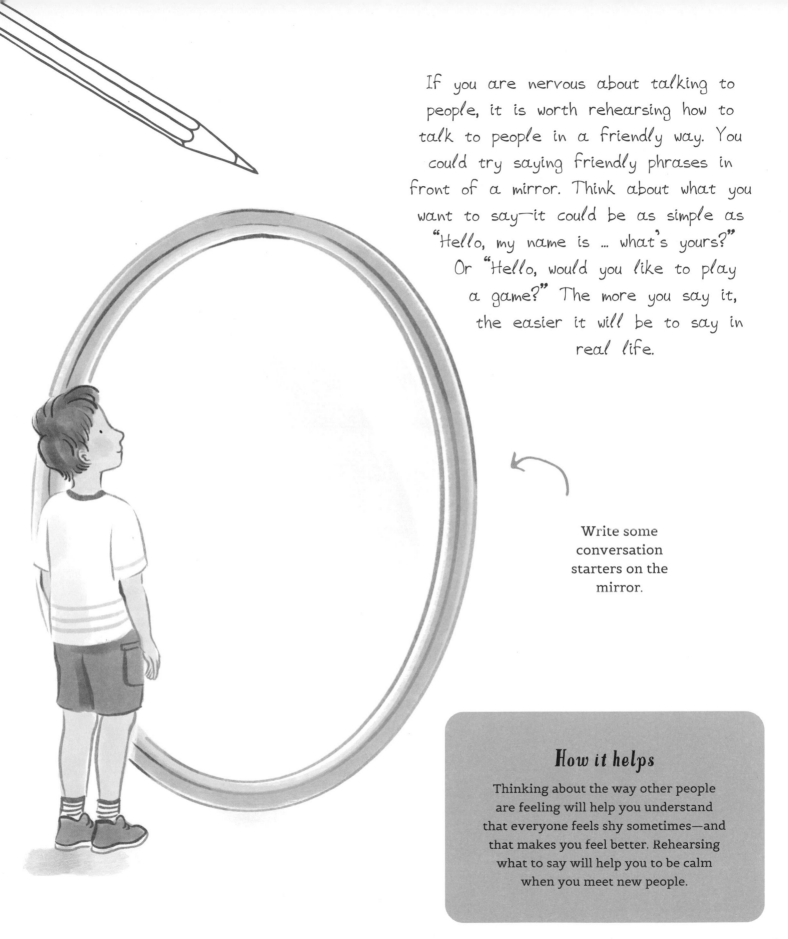

If you are nervous about talking to people, it is worth rehearsing how to talk to people in a friendly way. You could try saying friendly phrases in front of a mirror. Think about what you want to say—it could be as simple as "Hello, my name is ... what's yours?" Or "Hello, would you like to play a game?" The more you say it, the easier it will be to say in real life.

Write some conversation starters on the mirror.

How it helps

Thinking about the way other people are feeling will help you understand that everyone feels shy sometimes—and that makes you feel better. Rehearsing what to say will help you to be calm when you meet new people.

All Ears

Do you listen carefully when people speak? Or do you just wait for your turn to talk?

Do you know how to listen actively when somebody speaks to you? Active listening means you give them your full attention. Sometimes, we have lots of things we want to say, and it keeps us from listening properly. Instead, we just wait for a gap in the conversation so we can jump in and say something. It can be hard to stop yourself when you are excited.

If you are listening actively, you think about what the other person is saying and how they are feeling. Good listeners make great friends. They make people feel important and cared for.

Here are some signs of being a good listener:

Here are some signs that a person might not be a good listener:

Thinking about what the other person is saying

Yawning

Looking the person talking in the eye

Looking away

Nodding when you agree with things said

Interrupting and changing the subject

Can you think of some more signs to add to each list?

How it helps

Being a good listener will help you to make friends. Everyone wants to feel important and feel that what they say matters. Listening actively and commenting on what someone says will make them feel that you are a good friend to have.

Pay Attention!

An important part of making friends is finding out about the other person. What are their likes and dislikes?

It may be food, what they like to play, or places they like to go.

Become a friend detective, and try to notice and remember things about your new friend.

To remember what new friends like, try to imagine a bunch of balloons in the shape of the things they like. If they like cats, eating cookies, and playing ball games, think of them holding balloons in those shapes.

How it helps

When we remember things about people, it makes them feel that we care. We want to be with people that care about us and spend time with them. That can make us good friends.

Bodies Talk!

When we talk to people, they hear our voices—but they can also see what our bodies are "saying"!

When you talk to someone new, do you feel worried? If you do, your body might tell the person you are talking to how you are feeling. If you are worried, you may frown. You might cross your arms in front of you, or have bunched up shoulders. If your body looks worried, it can make the person you are talking to worry, too! Try and relax, and let your shoulders drop. Uncross your arms, and let them hang by your side.

Do you recognize the way people are feeling, even before they speak? Sometimes you can tell because of the way a person stands or how their face looks.

Look at the children in the pictures, and read their body language for clues about how they might be feeling.

How it helps

Being able to tell how people are feeling is a good way to interpret the situation and decide what action to take. Maybe you should leave them until they have calmed down, or maybe you should help them. Good friends try to make their friends feel better when they are sad or worried, for example.

Joining In

Joining in with a game can feel scary, but there are lots of ways to make it easier.

Start off by watching what the others are doing. Then ask yourself these questions:

What exactly is the point of the game?

How do people play it?

Look for ways you can fit in. If the game is playing at running a store, maybe you could join in by being a customer. Don't be pushy or try to change things—just play alongside the game as it is. You will soon become part of it!

Another good way to join in with a group is to see if there is a way that you can help with what they are doing. Maybe they are building a den or doing a job like raking leaves or picking up litter. These are activities that you could offer to help with. Doing things together like this is a great way to start new friendships.

How it helps

Working together to make something happen is a good way to join in with games and activities. If you show that you are helpful and useful, people will want you to join in all of the time!

Conversations Count

Making conversation is an important skill to learn. Watching how others talk to their friends can help you to come up with your own ideas.

When you go to a party with your family or go on an outing like the pool or the park, try to notice how grown-ups talk to their friends. Even adults can feel anxious about talking to people sometimes, but it is something they have learned to do. You can learn, too!

When grown-ups talk to each other, listen to what they say and how they say it. They probably share things about their lives and what they have been doing. They probably smile and chatter, asking questions about things like work and family members.

Try starting conversations with people you know, such as family members. This will give you a chance to work out your nerves in a safe space where people will be kind and reply. They will enjoy the attention, too!

Think of people you could start a conversation with. What could you talk about for each one? Draw them here in the photos, and write a list of things to talk about with each person.

How it helps

Watching people start conversations with people they don't know can give you ideas about trying it yourself—and rehearsing makes everything seem less scary!

Great Groups

If there's a group activity you'd like to try, but you are nervous about meeting new people, there are things you can try before jumping in completely.

Why not go along to watch activities before you join them? This will give you a chance to see if there are any children who look friendly taking part. Watch to see who helps people and makes kind comments. When you do feel brave enough to join in, go along early, before there are lots of people there. This will help you talk to one or two people at first—and those people could turn into friends!

If it's a school club, ask the teacher who runs it about who's in the club. Tell them that you feel a little shy about joining in—teachers are great at finding people to buddy up with, so you feel better. The buddy can help you understand how the group works and the activities they do, so that you don't feel awkward. Your buddy will know the other people in the group and can help you get to know them, too.

How it helps

Having a strategy for joining a group can make everything seem easier and friendlier. This will help you talk to new people without feeling awkward.

Write ideas for questions to ask about the group in the thought bubbles below.

One to One

Meeting one person for a play date at home can feel comfortable—so try it!

Even if you are anxious about making new friends, organizing a play date at home is a great idea. You are in a familiar place, so you feel comfortable there already. That will help you relax. Your family will be there, too, which makes you feel more secure. If anything gets awkward, they can help to smooth things over.

Ask a grown-up if you can plan a "pizza face" play date. You can buy pre-prepared bases and use tomato wedges, olives, pepper strips, and more to make happy faces on your pizzas—then eat them together!

Having something to do and talk about as you do it makes getting to know new people easier.

Where will I find people to invite?

You could invite someone from school, or your family might know other children who could come over to play. It might seem worrying at first, but soon you will wonder why you ever felt anxious. You can grow lots of friendships in this way—and even introduce your friends to each other so they make new friends, too!

How it helps

You can build a friendship group by meeting people one at a time. This can make you feel safe and secure as you learn things about new people, and they learn things about you.

Just Joking!

Telling funny jokes is a great way to make people relax—and it gives you something to say!

Do you like hearing jokes? We all like to laugh, and simple jokes can help to "break the ice" and make people relax. You can ask people if they want to hear a joke and tell one, and then ask if they know any. Laughing makes you feel good, and it's hard to feel nervous when you are laughing at something funny!

Try these ones:

Why do bees have sticky hair?

Because they use honey-combs!

What did the big flower say to the small flower?

Hi, bud!

What's orange and sounds like a parrot?

A carrot!

When someone is fun to be with, people want to spend time with them. Think about someone you know who is really fun. What do you like about them? How does being with them make you feel?

Think about ways to have fun. These are activities you can share with someone who comes to your house for a play date. Having fun will make them feel good, and they will want to come again, because being with you is fun.

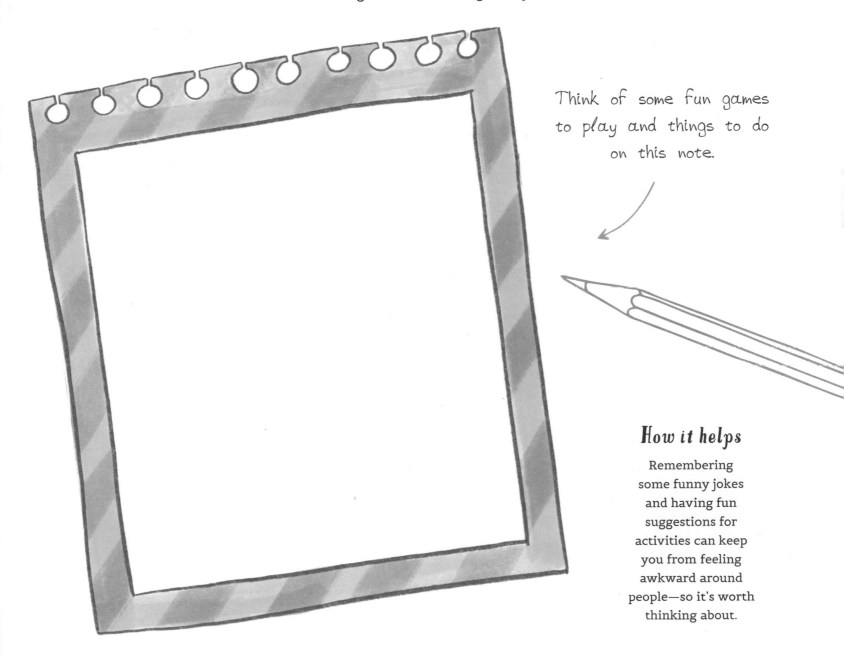

Think of some fun games to play and things to do on this note.

How it helps

Remembering some funny jokes and having fun suggestions for activities can keep you from feeling awkward around people—so it's worth thinking about.

Asking Questions

People really like being asked questions about themselves, and it's a great way to find out more about new people. When you find things that you both like, you have things to talk about and stories to share.

Do you like playing with puppets? Do you have any at home? Puppets are great for learning how to ask questions, because you or a family member can make them talk back! Why not think of some questions to ask your puppet (or a soft toy) about the things they like to do and play. Next time you meet somebody new, you'll know what to do.

An easy way to have a conversation is to ask somebody about the things they like best. You can ask about food, places, animals, clothes, books, songs … anything you can think of!

Don't forget to be ready with your own answers, too. Sharing things about yourself helps you get to know each other well.

Write the things you like best on the shapes. This will give you ideas of questions to ask new people, and it will help you prepare your own answers if they ask you back.

How it helps

Learning about each other is an important way to make a friendship grow. Sharing the things you like will help you get to know each other—and to see what you have in common.

Great Games

Having an idea bank of things to play will help you to feel more confident, and means you won't have to wonder "What can we do today?"

It is much easier to ask somebody to play with you if you have some ideas about what you can do together. Think about what games you like, and make a list of your ideas. They can be structured games, or they can be made-up games about pirate adventures and wizards!

When you have made your list of games, cut out some cards and write the best ideas on them. Find a little box or jar—ask a grown-up for one that you can use, or decorate an old package with bright paper. Put the cards inside, and add new ones when you think of, or hear about, new games. That way, your bank of games will keep growing, and you will never run out of things to do.

Have you ever played picture consequences? It's a really fun game to play with a new friend, because it makes people giggle!

Picture Consequences

You will need:
- A piece of paper for each player
- Pens and pencils

1. Each player draws a head at the top of the paper. Players fold the paper over, leaving only the neck showing, before passing their papers to the left.

2. Each player draws a body on their new piece of paper, starting from the neck. Players then fold the paper again, leaving just the tops of the legs showing. Papers are passed to the left.

3. This time, everyone draws legs and folds the paper, leaving just the bottoms of the legs, and passes on the paper.

4. Next, the players draw feet or shoes, fold, then pass the paper on.

5. Finally, each player opens them up to see the funny creations!

How it helps

Having a bank of ideas to look at means that you will always be ready with suggestions for things to play. You can use them to help you invite people to play with you— and when a friend is at your house, you can look in the bank together and let them choose something to do.

1.
Fold it over!

2.
And fold ...

3.
... one last fold!

4.

5.

Find the Clues

Use your puzzle-solving skills to figure out what things new people are interested in.

When you meet someone new, you can sometimes work out the things they like or are interested in by looking for the pieces of the puzzle that makes them "them!"

Do they wear hats often?

If they are wearing a character T-shirt, they might be interested in that cartoon or show.

Looks like this person likes red things!

What shape is their lunchbox? Maybe this person likes trucks!

Look at characters in books or magazines. What can you tell about them from the things they wear and the things they carry?

Write ideas about what they like or are interested in on the jigsaw pieces. What clues can you see?

Interesting Invitations

Every day, we have chances to invite people to do things. It's a great way to make new friends.

Invitations don't just have to be cards that ask you to birthday parties and celebrations. They can be simple things that we offer each other.

All of these things are kind, and they let people know that you are friendly.

Think about things you would like people to ask you to do. Are there times when you feel lonely? What would make you feel better? Think about things that you would like people to invite you to do—maybe you can invite somebody to do those things with you!

Write things you would like to be invited to do on these invitations.

How it helps

Thinking about ways to invite people to do things will help you make friends. If you spot someone looking lonely or lost, you can jump in with an invitation and make them feel better—and make a friend in the process.

What If?

When you are trying to make friends, thinking through things that might go wrong can take the sting out of your worries.

Playing a game of "What-if?" can help you look at the things that are making you anxious. If you are frightened of asking somebody to play with you, think of the best and worst things that could happen.

The best thing? They want to be your friend and play games with you.

The worst thing? You ask them to play, and they say no. If they don't want to play, you haven't lost anything. Think about what you would do if they said no. You'd probably just say "okay" and walk away. That's not so bad, is it?

If the first person you ask doesn't want to play with you, have a Plan B ready. What will you do next? A good idea might be to find someone else to ask. "What-ifs" give you the courage to keep trying.

Look at the "What-ifs" on these raindrops. Write what you would do if they happened on each ray of the Sun and dry up all of that rain!

What if I ask them to sit next to me for lunch, and they don't want to?

What if I ask them to play, and they say no?

What if I try to talk to them, and they ignore me?

How it helps

Thinking about "worst things" and deciding what you would do if they happened can make them seem a lot less scary. It can give you the confidence to try again!

Helping Friendships Grow

Have you ever grown flowers from seeds? Just like plants, friendships need care and attention to help them grow.

Smiling, saying hello, and inviting someone to join in with your game or play with your toys is like planting "friendship seeds."

It shows someone you want to be friends with them. Like seeds in the garden, sometimes they grow and sometimes they do not.

Plants need things to grow strong, such as sunshine, water, and good soil. We can help to make a friendship grow by giving it attention. That means doing things like being kind, listening, and sharing. Plants wither if they aren't looked after—and so do friendships!

Write the kind things you could do for a friend on the leaves of this friendship plant.

How it helps

It is important to understand that friendships need looking after to make them strong. Even grown-ups have to do this to make their friendships grow strong and healthy.

Sharing Is Caring

To be a good friend, you need to know how to share—it shows that you care.

Sharing the good things you have with your friends lets them know that you want them to have good things, too. That's an important part of friendship. You can share all kinds of things, like toys, food, games—and even clothes!

Think about all of the good things you have that you could share with a friend. Draw them on the shelf.

Sharing actual things is quite easy. Sharing ideas can be more complicated—but it's part of being a good friend. Sometimes you can feel shy about sharing your ideas. You can be worried that people might think your ideas are silly. A good friend will listen to your ideas with a "kind ear." This means they will not laugh at you, even if they don't agree. Sharing ideas with a friend can make you feel braver about sharing them with other people, perhaps at school.

How it helps

When you share things, and a friend shares their things with you, it makes your friendship feel stronger. It shows that you trust each other, and trust is very important.

Show Sympathy

We all need kindness when we are sad or hurt. Why not be a good friend and offer sympathy to a friend in need?

Sympathy means thinking about how another person is feeling and feeling sorry for them. Part of sympathy is wanting to make things better. If someone falls down and hurts their leg, a sympathetic person would help them get up and make sure they are okay. Good friends are sympathetic when their friend is hurt and in need of help and comfort.

You can also be a good friend by lending a sympathetic ear and listening when your friends are sad or anxious. Just like when they hurt their knee or feel unwell, you can listen and be kind. You can help your friend by telling a trusted grown-up, so that they get the help they need to feel better.

How it helps

Learning to be sympathetic is an important part of friendship. It makes people feel loved and cared for.

Can you think of sympathetic things to say? Write them so that this ear can "hear" them.

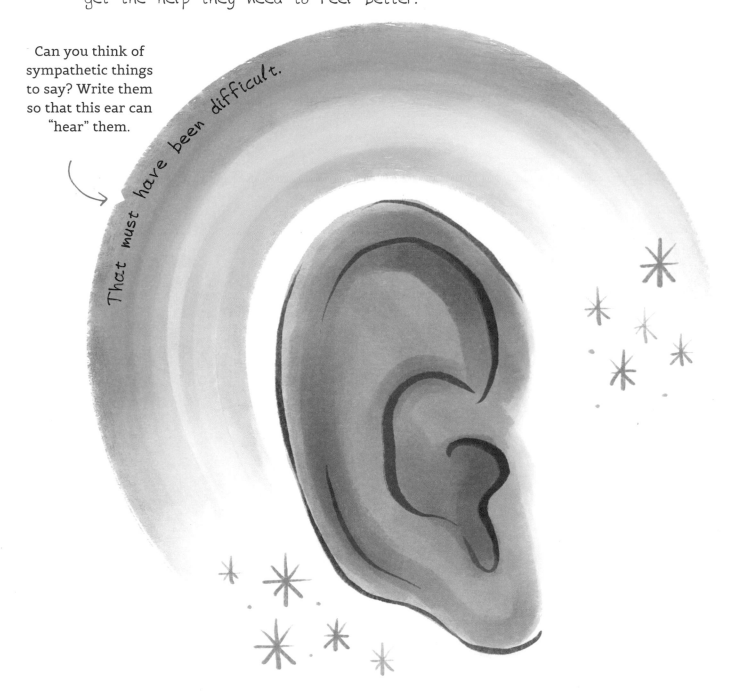

That must have been difficult.

Actions and Reactions

When we do things, there are always consequences. Make them good ones!

Everything we do makes things happen. If you do nice things for people, they feel happy. You can't always get things right, though, and everyone makes mistakes. Sometimes, you get things wrong, and people feel hurt. Being a good friend doesn't mean always doing the right thing—it means knowing how to fix things when they go wrong.

Imagine that you have said something when you were cross, and your friend is upset. What would you do to put things right? Write the things you would say to make things better on these rainbow hearts.

When we do nice things for people, it is like throwing a pebble into a pool. The ripples move outward, and they spread. If we are kind to people, they feel good and are likely to do nice things for us and other people. All this kindness can make new friendships begin and can make old friendships stronger.

Think of some kind things you could do, and write them on the ripples in the pool. Think how much kindness and friendship those ripples could create!

How it helps

To be a good friend, we need to remember that the things we do—kind or unkind—have an effect on our friends and our friendships, so we need to be careful and choose to be kind.

What Would You Do?

Friendships can be tricky at times—but if you plan for the worst, you'll often get the best.

No friends agree *all* of the time, because everyone is different. If you talk through your problems, you are less likely to argue. It is okay to disagree, as long as you are kind. That way, you can agree to have different viewpoints, and nobody needs to feel cross or hurt. A good way to make sure this happens often is to think through different situations in your head before they even happen! That means you are prepared and can be calm when your friend disagrees with you.

How it helps

Even friends don't agree all of the time. Figuring out what you would do in situations where you disagree will help you to decide on things to do and say, so that everyone is happy.

A great way to figure out how to deal with disagreements is to role-play with a grown-up that you trust. It could be a teacher or relative. Use these "problem" cards to figure out what you would do and say in each situation. Your grown-up can act the part of your friend.

1. You want to play outside, but your friend wants to stay inside.

2. Your friend wants to do something that you don't think is safe.

3. You want to watch a cartoon, but your friend wants to watch another show.

4. Your friend wants to play computer games, but you don't enjoy it.

Why Did They Do That?

Thinking about the reasons why people do the things they do can help you to be a good friend.

When somebody does something you do not like, it is too easy to think they are being mean or nasty. If you take a moment to think it through, they probably have a reason for the way they acted—even if what they did was not right.

When people are sad or cross, they sometimes lash out and say things they don't mean. If you figure out the reason they might have been feeling bad, you might understand why they said something unkind. That doesn't make it okay to say nasty things, but it can help you to understand.

Try to think of the last time you were feeling cross. Did you say or do anything at the time and feel sorry later? Your friend might be feeling that way, too.

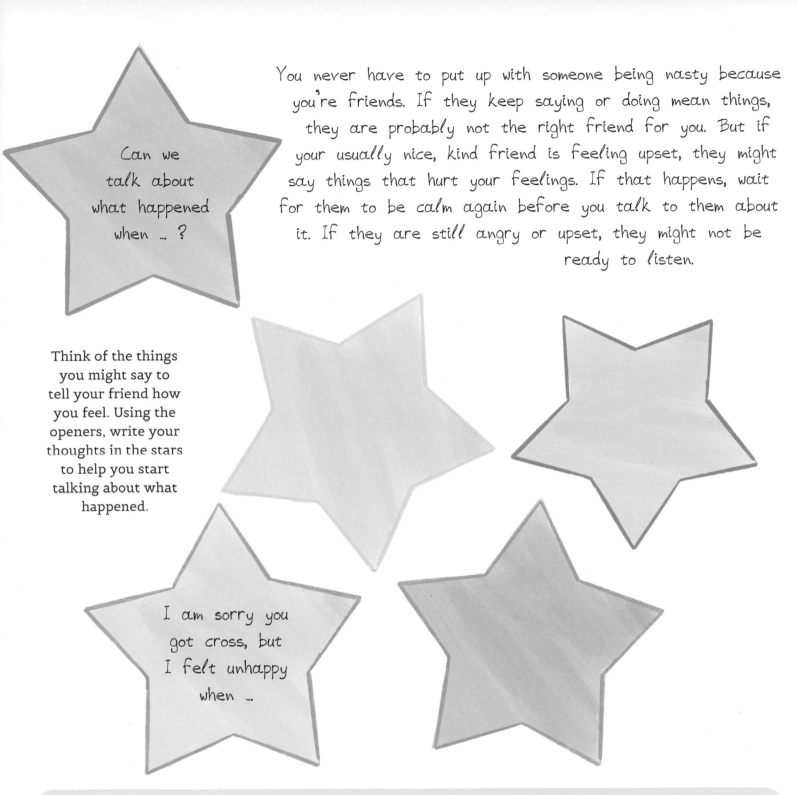

Can we talk about what happened when … ?

You never have to put up with someone being nasty because you're friends. If they keep saying or doing mean things, they are probably not the right friend for you. But if your usually nice, kind friend is feeling upset, they might say things that hurt your feelings. If that happens, wait for them to be calm again before you talk to them about it. If they are still angry or upset, they might not be ready to listen.

Think of the things you might say to tell your friend how you feel. Using the openers, write your thoughts in the stars to help you start talking about what happened.

I am sorry you got cross, but I felt unhappy when …

How it helps

Figuring out what to say and do when things go wrong is an important part of friendship. Remember to tell a trusted grown-up what happened, and talk through what you are going to say and do to make things feel better.

Oops! Sorry ...

Part of being a good friend is learning to say sorry when you need to.

Sometimes, saying sorry can make you feel uncomfortable or even angry. It's especially hard when you don't feel as though you need to say sorry. The thing is, saying sorry makes people feel better. If grown-ups ask you to say sorry, it usually means they want you to think about what you have done. Now, think about how that applies to friendship. Has a friend ever done something that made you feel upset? Maybe they left you out of something. Chances are they didn't realize you would be upset and didn't mean to hurt you.

It is important to mean it when you say sorry. If you have done something you regret, just saying "sorry" is not always enough. To make friends (and family!) feel better, it is better to make an active apology. Say sorry, but also try to put the thing you did wrong right again. If you left someone out of an activity, say sorry and that you did not mean to hurt their feelings. Then ask the person to do something nice with you to make up for leaving them out. They might still feel a little sad about what happened, but it will show them that you have thought about what you did and are truly sorry.

Did not share toys

Left friend out of a game

Look at the problems on the flowers, and write ideas for active apologies on the labels.

Forgot friend's birthday

How it helps

Apologies should be actions as well as words, because active apologies let friends know you understand how they are feeling. Everyone makes mistakes sometimes, don't worry!

Keeping Calm

When you are making new friends or playing with old friends, problems can arise.
There are lots of ways to stay calm and talk things through.

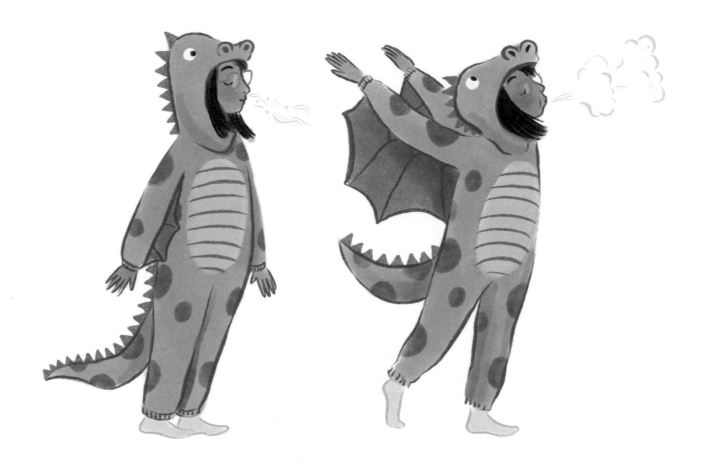

If you are feeling worried or upset, taking a deep breath can really help you stay calm. It floods your body with fresh air, so that you can keep a clear head—and it keeps you from saying anything too quickly that you might regret! Breathing slowly and calmly will help you relax, and it will give you time to think. Try to imagine breathing in sparkles through your nose and breathing out puffs of clouds through your mouth. When you are calm again, you will be able to think about ways to solve the problem.

It helps to walk away if you feel too upset to speak kindly. You can also imagine yourself standing under a cool waterfall. Think about the water pouring down and taking the heat of your upset feelings down into the ground with it. When you feel cool and calm again, you will be able to think more clearly about ways to solve the problem you were having.

Look at this waterfall. Circle the words you think should flow down and sink into the ground.

cross

argue

smile

angry

kind

scowl

hurtful

happy

How it helps

Thinking about ways to calm down will give you the tools to cope when you get frustrated. They will give you the space to think before you say things that could hurt somebody.

Solving Problems Together

When there are problems and disagreements, it's important to be able to talk about them and solve them.

After there has been an argument or disagreement and you have calmed down, you need to talk about the problem. You need to solve it, not ignore it. It won't go away on its own. Make sure that you use kind words to talk about problems. Don't start arguing again. Say how you felt without blaming the other person. Then listen to them as they say how they felt. You both probably felt hurt at the same time—and that's why the argument happened.

For this activity, you need a family member to role-play with. Imagine that you have been angry because you argued with somebody. Perhaps you said you thought they were being silly, and they got upset with you. Imagine that you have come to talk to them to make things right. Start out by apologizing, then talk about how you could have done things in a different way, without having an argument. Your family member might have some ideas to share about how they have dealt with conflict between friends. We can learn from each other!

How it helps

We all need to learn how to sort out problems and soothe hurt feelings. Learning to use kind words can help us make ourselves and others comfortable and happy again after an argument.

Friendship Library

Stories can help you learn about how friendship works and how people make friends.

Do you like reading? Next time you go to the library or a bookshop, hunt for books about friendships. You will be amazed at how many there are! The friends inside may be children, grown-ups, or even animals, but the things you can learn about friendship from reading their stories are useful either way. As you read, think about different ways the characters are showing that they are (or are not!) being good friends to each other.

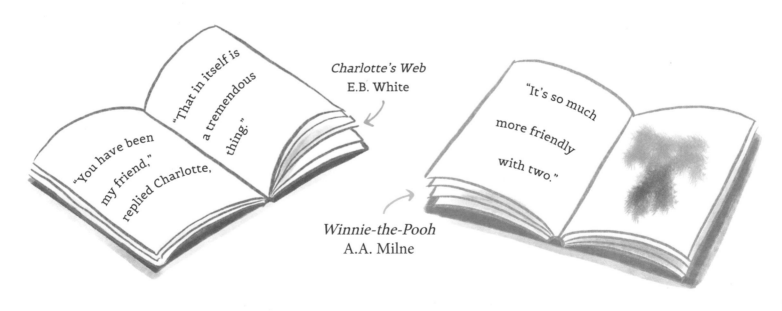

"You have been my friend," replied Charlotte, "That in itself is a tremendous thing."

Charlotte's Web
E.B. White

"It's so much more friendly with two."

Winnie-the-Pooh
A.A. Milne

You can even write your own friendship book. It can be a story about friends or a nonfiction book that talks all about friendship—just like this one. Make a book out of folded paper and a card cover, or use a notebook. If you are making up a story about some friends, you might want to plan your ideas out on scrap paper first. If you are writing a nonfiction book, you might want to just fill in the pages as you get ideas. Make sure you draw fabulous pictures to go with your writing.

How it helps

Learning about how lots of different friendships work is a good way to think about what you want your friendships to be like. Some of the stories might give you lovely ideas about things to do with friends.

Playing by the Rules

It's sometimes hard to make sure you aren't being bossy when you play with a group—but it's worth it in terms of friendship.

When you are playing a game—especially if it is one you have made up—it can be hard not to try and make all of the rules. You can get excited and take over. Some people don't get a chance to share their ideas, and that can make them feel bad. The thing is, people don't like to play with bossy people because it feels as though their ideas—and they themselves—don't count. So if you are prone to taking charge, be careful that doesn't spill over into being bossy.

How it helps

We all need to learn to listen to each other's ideas. If everyone takes a turn talking about their ideas, it makes them feel important and like their ideas count.

When you are figuring out ways to play a game, especially with new people, it's important to take turns sharing your ideas about how the game should work. Everyone thinks their own ideas are best in the beginning, but if you listen to other people, good things happen. They feel heard, and they might have some great ideas that make the game even better.

Think about some gentle ways to share ideas when you are deciding how to play a game. What could you say? Write your ideas on these Ideas cards. The first one has been done for you.

Idea

What do you think we should do first?

Idea

Idea

Idea

Idea

Idea

Develop your Kindness Muscles

When it comes to friendship, kindness might be what matters most.

If you spend time around kind people, it tends to rub off on you. This means that we learn good habits from each other. Try to notice all the kind things that you see happening around you each day.

The great thing about kindness is that it can grow like strong muscles. The more often we do kind things, the more our kindness grows. Every kind act makes our "kindness muscles" grow stronger and work better.

How it helps

Thinking about kind acts and how to be kind will help you to be a good friend and helper to everyone—whether they are part of your group of friends or not. If they weren't before, they may want to be your friend because you are so kind!

Kindness keeps you warm, like a soft quilt. Offering kindness makes you feel happy inside, and when people are kind to you, it makes you feel good, too. Look at this Kindness Quilt. Write a kind action on each of the squares. Think about times when people have called you kind—what had you done? Think about times when people have been kind to you. What did they do?

Caring Compliments

We all like to hear nice things said about us. Complimenting someone can give them a really strong confidence boost.

How do you feel when somebody gives you a compliment? It makes most people feel happy and proud. Imagine someone saying how well you sing or how great you are at writing neatly. How would that feel? It's a good feeling—and we want our friends to feel good. Telling friends honestly that they are good at things is a great way to make them feel confident.

Try and find something nice to say to someone every day. Make sure you notice what your friends are good at. It's important to tell people the things you like about them. It's also important to notice the things that you are good at and what you like about yourself. It's like giving yourself a compliment!

Draw a picture of yourself in this mirror. Then write down four things you like about yourself.

How it helps

Getting compliments that are truly meant is the perfect way to build confidence. That is the same for other people—and the compliments you give yourself!

Have Empathy

Empathy is thinking about and understanding why people feel the way they do. If we have empathy, we understand why people feel the way they do, because we can imagine how it would feel. It's good to have—and be—a friend with empathy.

Empathy is important because it shows people that you understand how they are feeling and that you care. If a friend is feeling sad, a person with empathy knows what it is like to feel sad and uses their experiences to make their friend feel supported. Empathy doesn't make you "fix" things for your friend, but it does show them that they are not alone. It's important to be there for someone when they need you.

Read the statements on the opposite page. Draw a face to show how you would feel if these things happened to you. Then read the statements to a friend or family member, and ask them to make a face to show how they would feel. Does it look like the face you drew?

A good friend can look at things from your point of view, even if they don't feel the same way or agree with you. They can understand how something might affect you, even if it would not affect them in the same way. If you want to be a good friend, you should try and see things from your friend's point of view.

How it helps

Thinking about empathy will help you develop strong friendships. If you try to see things from other people's point of view, it will help you to be understanding and kind.

You tripped up and hurt your knee.	

You saw a video of yourself in the school play.	

You looked in the mirror and realized you had food stains around your mouth—and they had been there for hours!	

A trip you were looking forward to didn't go ahead due to bad weather.	

Your friend got a toy for their birthday that you have wanted for a long time.	

You heard a spooky noise during the night.	

When Friendships Fade

Friendships don't always last forever because people change and grow—and that's okay.

Over time, friendships change. Sometimes you stay friends with people you have known since preschool. Other times, people change and friendships fade. Nothing goes wrong exactly. There's no argument or harsh words. As people grow and change, they sometimes develop new interests that some of their friends don't share. These friends can start to drift away, and we don't realize until they are gone. We stop seeing them. That can be a natural part of life.

Sometimes, friendships change because the people develop in different ways and have different values. Sometimes, you can even find that old friends become unpleasant to be around. Maybe they have a new group of friends and behave in a way that you don't find comfortable. That's okay, too—it happens because life changes. As these friends drift away—or we move away from them—it gives us the space to make new friends that share our values such as being kind and honest.

How it helps

Recognizing that sometimes friendships fade is an important part of growing up. We can think about our memories with that friend and smile, but still know that our lives have changed and we have drifted apart.

Friendship Checklist

Creating a friendship checklist can help you to make sure that the friendships you have are healthy, happy, and right for you.

Friendship Checklist

I feel listened to. ☐

I feel looked after. ☐

_____ ☐

_____ ☐

_____ ☐

_____ ☐

_____ ☐

_____ ☐

Good friendships are good for both of the people in them. This means that both people feel supported, looked after, listened to, and cared about. It's good to check from time to time that your friendships are good ones. If one person is doing all the caring, it's not a good friendship!

Make your own friendship checklist. What will you include? Write the things that are most important to you on this list. Some have been written for you.

From time to time, you should think about how healthy your friendships are. Do both of you do nice things for each other? Do you both check that the other is okay? Do you have fun together, but also share your problems? If so, you are equal partners, and you have a healthy friendship. If not, think of ways you can both change that.

How it helps

Thinking carefully about your friendships from time to time can help you stay good friends, because both people feel important to the other.

Friendship High Five

How can you be a good friend? There are lots of different ways to become the best friend anyone could ever ask for.

Really good friends make you feel so happy that you want to give them a high five! Look at the ideas on the hands, and think about ways to be a good friend.

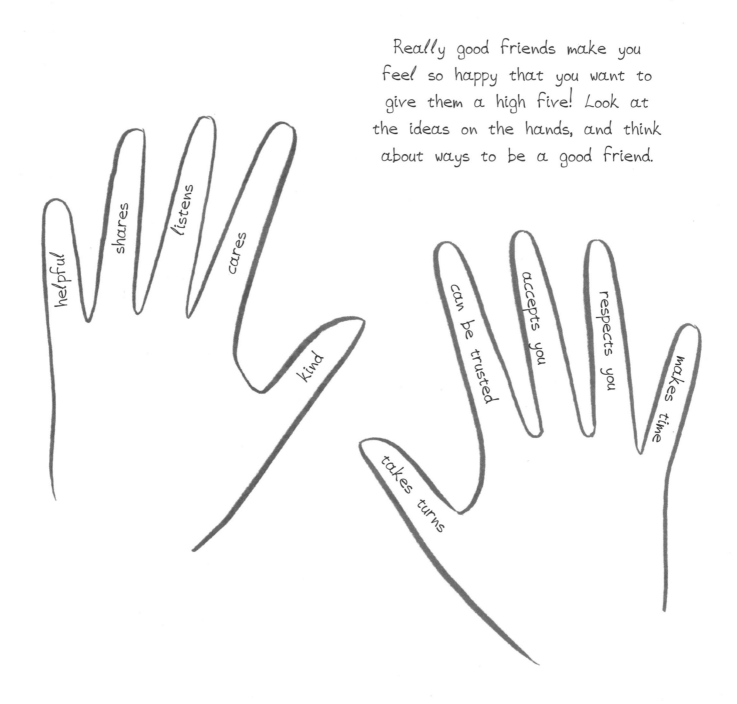

Find some bright paper, and draw around your hand. What do you think makes a good friend? You can use some of the ideas on the hands or think of your own ideas. Cut out the hand, then write your good friend ideas on the fingers.

You could ask your friends to do the same and see if your ideas are similar. If they are, you have a friendship "high five"! If they are different, talk about how. It's good to find out what other people feel about things.

How it helps

Thinking about what makes a good friend will help you to make sure your friendships are good—for you AND your friends! Being able to discuss things like this will help you your whole life long—even when you are a grown-up.

For Parents and Carers

Why does my child find it hard to make friends?

Today, it feels as though every moment of our children's lives are planned and mapped. That can make finding time for friendship hard. There are so many opportunities for activities outside school that it can feel as though we are constantly shuttling the children from place to place. When we were children, we spent lots of our time playing outside with local kids after school—and that can feel like it has become a thing of the past in many places.

Downtime is an important part of the ability to grow friendships. This encourages chatting freely, inventing and playing games together, and especially negotiating the rules about how a game works. If our children don't have any unstructured or curated downtime (away from screens) it can be hard for them to find the space to make friends.

It's important to build in opportunities for your child to have these experiences if there are no organic opportunities for them to do so. Taking the first step is often the hardest part of making friends, and children (as well as many adults) can become quite socially anxious as a result. The more anxious they get, the harder it becomes to speak to someone new—and this becomes a self-perpetuating problem.

Make sure you notice opportunities for your child to make friends. They don't all have to come from school or be exactly the same age as your child. If you think about your own group of friends, there will be people of different ages from diverse settings. You have coworkers, local friends, parent friends from your child's school, friends from a book club … your child can make friends in the same way.

Do you have coworkers with children around the same age? You could invite families over for a barbecue or a picnic. You could approach other parents to take turns hosting parties, so the children can play together. Suggest carpooling to families whose children go to clubs with your children. Arriving together, after talking in the car, gives them a head start in sharing their activity together, and friendship could grow. Likewise, riding home together creates a common bond and gives them time to cement a friendship.

When to get professional help

If your child seems consistently lonely despite your efforts to help their situation, it may be time to time to think about seeking professional help. It may be useful to arrange to speak to your child's teacher at school. They will be able to give you their overview of how your child socializes at school and offer them help in the school setting. They may also be able to give you the contact details of school or community support groups. If you are worried about your child, a visit to your family doctor may be helpful to talk about your worries, and perhaps to access social skills training.

For Parents

How you can help

1. Be ready to talk with your child when they need to work out worries or problems about making friends, or friendships.

Try to be casual and calm—kids pick up quickly on any tension or anxiety from you. Be an active listener, gently prompting your child where necessary to help them express their thoughts and ideas. Make sure that they are relaxed by talking at "incidental" family times—when preparing or eating meals together or when driving them to activities, for example. This approach makes the conversation feel less loaded than sitting down specifically to talk.

2. Arrange casual play dates for your child, so that they are not under pressure to make friends.

Invite school or club friends along on family outings, and make casual after-school dates on a regular basis. These casual encounters help to normalize social situations and dampen any anxiety your child may be feeling. Many of your own acquaintances may have children who could make pleasant companions for your child.

3. Talk about your childhood friends.

Tell stories—not just the glowingly happy stories about childhood parties and picnics or trips to the beach, but also stories about times when you disagreed or argued, but worked on your relationship. This will help your child understand that friendships can survive, even when there have inevitably been disagreements. Friendships have ups and downs and are rarely perfect. If your child is reassured that this is the case, it may help them form and manage their own friendships.

4. Model friendships for your child.

Let them "catch" you being a good friend, checking in on friends who are having problems, for example, or buying small, fun gifts to cheer their day. Talk positively about your friends and their kindness toward you.

Good luck with your work presentation this afternoon! XOXO

How to use this book

Dip into this book to find actual hands-on, practical ways to help your child make friends and maintain friendships. The book is not meant to be worked through step by step, but the handy activities and tips can help when your child needs that extra reassurance that they can manage issues that their friendships—or lack of them—might create. This book offers gentle, easy-to-understand activities that will help your child to approach friendship with an open heart and mind.

For Parents

How you can help (continued)

5. Find a club that your child might like to join where they can meet like-minded friends.
They may like bugs, for example, and want to join a young entomologists club. They may be very sporty and like to join a youth sports club. They may enjoy joining an art club. These options offer opportunities to casually talk to and befriend other children without pressure as worries about what to say are reduced by ready-made, club-specific topics.

6. Actively "notice" and refer to children in your child's circle (whether at school, at a club, or the child of a family friend) who seem friendly.
Forcing the issue will not work, but casually mentioning how nice and friendly somebody is may just give your child the prompt they need to approach someone. Remember to follow their lead and separate your feelings about their friendship status from theirs. You are your child's coach, but you don't have a horse in the race!

7. If your child is feeling shy, do not cajole them into joining in or taking part in a play session or game.

It may make them feel panicked or trapped. Instead, strew opportunities for meeting people in their path by going to the playground, a park, or a community event together. In this low-pressure way, opportunities for making friendships will develop more naturally for your child.

8. Try and avoid projecting your feelings onto your child.

Just because you were popular and outgoing (or not) at school, it doesn't mean your child will be the same way. Consider the fact that your child may be really happy with a small friendship group, and they may not want to make lots of friends. As long as they are friendly to other children, that may be enough.

For Parents

How you can help (continued)

9. Scaffold play dates with new people, especially if your child is shy or anxious. This means organizing an activity that involves each child in the process as it plays out.

For example, you could set up a "cooking play date" where you offer ingredients to make a pizza or build ice cream sundaes. Asking the children open-ended questions that require opinions about the activities as they unfold can help create a low-key discussion and make both children involved feel comfortable and empowered.

10. Check in from time to time with your child about their friendships.

Make it a normal part of life to chat about how their friends are, what they are doing, etc. This makes thinking through and working on friendship a habit and part of daily life. It it also gives your child a regular, low-stakes way to talk through any issues or problems without it becoming a big deal.

11. It is important to take an interest in your child's friends and activities, so that you can keep an overview of their welfare when they are out of your care.

Some friends may be a better influence than others in terms of actions and worldviews, and if there are issues that arise from your chats, you can discuss them calmly and ask "What would you do in those circumstances?" Talking things through and being involved rather than banning particular friendships (which will only make them more attractive) is increasingly important as your child grows older. Discussing good decisions is a great way to model safe actions as your child moves out of the realm of your influence as they grow.

12. Help your child to become emotionally literate.

Talk about feelings gently; offer child-friendly anecdotes from your own life. Talk about what a good friend is and how they behave. In an age-appropriate manner, introduce ideas of less than comfortable "friendships," such as where friends do not listen, or try to coerce—or even bully—their friendship group into doing things. Learning to identify unsupportive friendships helps children avoid them.

Glossary

activity
Something that you do, such as a game, sport, or craft.

anxious
Feeling worried.

attention
Taking notice of something.

body language
The way someone moves, stands, and acts that shows the way they are feeling.

comfort
Something that makes you feel better, such as a hug when you are sad.

confidence
A feeling of security in yourself and belief in your own abilities.

conversation
When two or more people talk together.

disagreement
An argument.

dislike
When you find something unpleasant.

empathy
When you understand how someone is feeling because you know how you would feel if the same thing happened to you.

frustration
Feeling upset and angry because you cannot do something or because something does not work the way it should

greetings
Ways to say hello.

interests
Subjects that capture your attention and you spend time learning about.

interpret
To be able to understand and decode the actions of others.

kindness
Being helpful, gentle, and thinking of the needs of others

play date
Getting together to play or do an activity together with a friend.

polite
Saying "please" and "thank you" and acting in a way that shows you care about the way other people are feeling.

signal
A way to show somebody something.

situation
Something that happens.

sympathy
Being and understanding when someone has a problem or is feeling sad.

uncomfortable
Feeling awkward.

understand
When something happens and you can see why it has happened.

upset
Feeling unhappy.

viewpoints
Different ways of looking at things or situations.

Further Reading

Books

Growing Friendships: A Kids' Guide to Making and Keeping Friends by Eileen Kennedy-Moore and parenting and health writer Christine McLaughlin

Social Skills Activities for Kids: 50 Fun Exercises for Making Friends, Talking and Listening, and Understanding Social Rules by Natasha Daniels

The Children's Book of Making Friends by Sophie Giles

The Survival Guide to Making and Being Friends by James J. Crist

How to Talk With Friends: A Step-by-Step Social Skills Curriculum for Children with Autism by Janine Toole

The Teenage Guide to Friends by Nicola Morgan

North America

verywellfamily.com/
This parenting website has some useful tips on making and keeping friends.

childmind.org/
The Child Mind Institute's website is a useful mental health resource for parents and carers.

embracerace.org/resources/why-and-how-to-encourage-cross-racial-friendships-among-children
This article has ideas for encouraging diverse friendships.

understood.com
Understood advises and supports families of children who learn and think differently. Its website provides resources on a variety of issues including loneliness and social anxiety.

UK

youngminds.org.uk/
This charity provides support and resources for young people suffering with mental health issues.

mindedforfamilies.org.uk/
MindEd provides information for parents and carers about the mental health of children.

childline.org.uk
Free call: 0800 1111
Childline offers help and advice on a huge range of issues with free, confidential counselling by email, online chat, and telephone.

Australia and New Zealand

Kidshelpline.com.au/ or call 1800551800
This organization provides telephone and online counselling for young people aged 5–25.

raisingchildren.net.au/

youthline.co.nz
Free call 080037633
Free text 234

Index

A

actions and reactions 58–9
active listening 26–7, 88
anger 62–3, 67, 69
anxious feelings 5, 17, 24–5, 34, 38, 57, 87–8, 92
apologies 64–5, 68–9
arguments 60–5, 68–9
attention, paying 28–9

B

body language 30–1
books, friendship 70–1
bossy people 72–3
breathing techniques 66

C

calmness 16, 24–5, 60, 66–7, 88
caring approaches 82–3
checklist, friendship 82–3
clubs 11, 37, 90
comforting others 56–7
compliments 76–7
confidence 16, 17, 51, 76–7
consequences 58–9
conversation skills 14, 24–5, 34–5, 42–3

D

developing friendships 52–3
difference 13, 22–3
difficulties making friends 86–7
disagreements 60–5, 68–9
downtime 86

E

emotions
  anger 62–3, 67, 69
  emotional literacy 93
  projection 91
  recognition 30–1
empathy 78–9
ending friendships 80–1

F

finding friendship 4–5

G

games 44–5
  games banks 44–5
  invitations to play 50–1
  joining in 14–17, 32–3
  rules 72–3
good friends 4, 21
greetings 8–9, 52
group activities, trying out 36–7

H

hello, learning how to say 8–9, 52
helping others 6–7, 33

I

ideas, sharing 55, 72–3
  interests
  finding out about people's 46–7
shared 11, 12–13, 47
invitations 48–9, 50–1

J

joining in 14–17, 32–3, 91
jokes 40–1

K

kindness 6–7, 59, 74–5, 78, 89

L

lashing out 62–3
left out, feeling 14–15, 65
listening skills 26–7, 57, 82, 88
loneliness 4–5, 49, 87

M

motivations, understanding other people's 62–3

N

nasty actions 63

O

one-to-one contact 38–9

P

parent's guide 86–93
Picture Consequences (game) 45
pizza-making 38
places to meet 10–11, 87
play dates 38–9, 88, 92
problem-solving 68–9
professional help 87
puppets 42

Q

qualities, friendship 20–1, 84–5
questions, asking 42–3

R

rejection, coping with 50–1
role models 7
role-play 61, 69
rules 72–3

S

sadness 4, 31, 56–7, 62, 64, 66, 78
sharing 54–5, 65
shyness 91, 92
smiling 8–9, 52
sympathy 56–7

T

talking things through 88–9, 92–3
turn-taking 72–3
types of friendship 22–3

W

"What-if?" thinking 50–1
worries 30, 50–1, 66, 88